D1716150

THE TREASURE BOOK

—OF—

CHILD'S POEMS.

LITTLE WILL

AND OTHER STORIES.

1878.

Republished by:
ANGELA'S BOOK SHELF
9746 N. Mason Road
Wheeler, MI 48662

Contents.

Little Will.

A GREAT crowd of people had
gathered around
A small ragged urchin stretched
out on the ground
In the midst of the street; and some
cried, "For shame!"
And others, "Can any one tell us his
name?"
For that poor little body, now bleeding
and still,
Was all that was left of once bright
little Will.
A great heavy cart had come rattling
that way,

Where Willie and others were busy at
    play,
And the poor little fellow, now stretched
    on the stones,
Seemed only a mass of bruised flesh and
    crushed bones.
But still there was life; and a kind
    doctor said,
"We must take the child home and put
    him to bed.
He must have all the care we can pos-
    sibly give,
And it may be the poor little fellow
    will live."

But alas for poor Willie! he *had* no nice
    home;
He lived in an alley, in one little room;
And his poor mother, working from
    earliest light,
Had often no supper to give him at
    night.
But joy for poor Willie! for not far
    away
From the place where all bleeding and
    shattered he lay,

Is a very large house standing back from
the street,
With everything 'round it so quiet and
neat,
Which many good people had built in
His name
Who healed all the sick when from
Heaven he came,
And who promises blessings that ever
endure,
To those who shall comfort the sick and
the poor.

So there in a room, large and cheerful
and bright,
Little Willie was laid on a pillow so
white.
The walls with bright pictures were
covered all o'er;
Will never had seen such a clean place
before.
Long rows of small beds, with small
tables between,
The coverlids white, and the beds
painted green;

And so many children, all sick, but so
    bright,
Will almost forgot his great pain at the
    sight.

But the poor little boy suffered terrible
    pain
When the good surgeon came to ex-
    amine again
Those poor little limbs; and he said
    that next day
He must bring his sharp knife and cut
    both legs away.
Oh! how could he bear it? Oh! what
    should he do?
So small, and alone, he could never get
    through.
And then he knew well that he never
    could run,
And play with the boys, as before he
    had done.
Poor Willie! he felt that in all that
    great city,
There was no one to help him and no
    one to pity.

It was night; in the hospital ward all
    was still,
Save the low moans of anguish from poor
    little Will,
When a dear little girl in the very next
    bed
Turned round on her pillow and lovingly
    said,

" Little boy, what's the matter; are you
    very ill ? "
" Oh ! yes ! " said poor Willie; " and
    what is worse still,
The doctor is going to hurt my leg so
To-morrow; I never can bear it, I
    know."
" But Jesus will help you," said dear
    little Sue;
" He suffered and died, you know,
    Willie, for you."
The child was astonished, and thus
    made reply:
" Why, Susie, who's Jesus? and what
    made him die ? "
" O Willie, how sad! I thought every
    one knew.

You do n't go to Sabbath-school, is n't
    that true?"
" No, I never have been," the boy made
    reply;
" But tell me of Jesus, and what made
    him die."

" Well, Jesus," said Susie, " came down
    long ago,
Because he was sorry we all suffered
    so,
And would be so naughty. And he was
    a child,
Just as little as we, but so gentle and
    mild.
And when he grew up he went all
    through the land,
And healed all the sick with the touch
    of his hand;
And he took little children right up on
    his knee—
O Willie, I wish it had been you and
    me.
But soon cruel men caught Jesus one
    day,

And beat him, and mocked him, and
    took him away,
And nailed him with nails to a great
    cross of wood.
Oh! wasn't it hard when he'd done
    them such good?
How he must have loved us to die on
    the tree."
" But," said Will, " if he's dead, how can
    he help *me*?"
" Why, I'll tell you," said Susie;
    " though now he's in Heaven,
In the Book he has left us a promise is
    given,
That whene'er we want him he'll come
    to our aid.
I'm so sure he loves me, I'm never
    afraid.
I know that he comes to this hospital
    here;
And though folks can't *see* him, they
    feel he is near.
I know, for I've tried it again and
    again,
He helps us bear sickness, and sorrow,
    and pain."

"Oh, how good!" said the boy, with a
    long, thankful sigh.
"But I am so small that he might pass
    me by;
So I'll put up my hand, just so he can
    see,
Then he'll know that I want him, and
    come right to me."
When the bright sun peeped in on that
    little white bed,
The hand was still raised, but dear
    Willie was dead!
The sad look of pain had gone from his
    face,
And the sweetest of smiles had taken
    its place;
For far off in Heaven, that beautiful
    land,
Kind Jesus had seen little Will's lifted
    hand;
The smile on his face Jesus' kissing had
    given,
And he'll wake in the morning with
    Jesus in Heaven.
Dear friends who have read this sweet
    story, you see

That trusting in Jesus will save you
    and me.
Oh! that all who of Jesus' great mercy
    have heard,
Would, like dear little Willie, *take him
    at his word.*

THE CUP-BEARER.

THE little cup-bearer entered the room,
    After the banquet was done;
His eyes were like the skies of May,
    Aglow with the cloudless sun.
Kneeling beside his master's feet,
    The feet of the noble king,
He raised the goblet. "Drink, my liege,
    The offering that I bring."

"Nay, nay," the good king smiling said,
    "But first a faithful sign

That thou bringest me no poison draught:
   Taste thou, my page, the wine."
Then gently, firmly, spoke the lad,
   " My dearest master, no,
Though at thy slightest wish my feet
   Shall gladly come and go."

" Rise up, my little cup-bearer,"
   The king astonished cried;
" Rise up and tell me straightway, Why
   Is my request denied?"
The young page rose up slowly,
   With sudden paling cheek,
While courtly lords and ladies
   Waited to hear him speak.

" My father sat in princely halls,
   And tasted wine with you.
He died a wretched drunkard, sire—"
   The brave voice tearful grew;
" I vowed to my dear mother,
   Beside her dying bed,

That for her sake I would not taste
   The tempting poison red."

" Away with this young upstart ! "
   The lords impatient cry ;
But spilling slow the purple wine,
   The good king made reply :
" Thou shalt be my cup-bearer,
   And honored well," he said,
" But see thou bring not wine to me,
   But water pure instead."

WHERE'ER in life thy path may lead,
   Always make truth thy guide ;
Let not the wealth of royal mines
   Entice thee from her side.
Oh, from her bright and pleasant ways
   Let not thy steps depart ;
Better than gold or brilliant gems,
   A pure and guileless heart.

LITTLE SUNSHINE.

THEY call me Little Sunshine,
　　I'm sure I can't tell why;
I'm not at all like the great sun,
　　That lives up in the sky.

He is traveling all the day,
　　And shines for every one;
I do n't know what we all would do
　　If he did n't ever come.

I love to see his great round face,
　　'Fore he goes to bed at night;
I guess he's getting tired then,
　　He does n't shine so bright.

And when he's gone behind the trees,
　　And stars begin to peep,
Then mamma takes me in her arms,
　　And lets me go to sleep.

(18)

When I wake in the morning,
  His face is bright and red;
And he's looking through the window,
  Right on my trundle-bed.

I love so much to have him shine,
  He makes it warm and light;
He makes the little dew-drops
  Sparkle so very bright.

Sometimes I go to grandma's,
  I can't tell all I do;
I play so nice with Uncle Ned,
  He calls me Sunshine, too.

And then I sit on grandpa's knee—
  He tells so many things—
Stories about the beasts and birds,
  And fairies that have wings.

Grandma has some little birdies,
  I helped her give them food.
I love my grandma very much
  Because she is so good,

There is so much at grandma's
  It makes me very glad;
But when I think of mamma,
  I'm just a little sad.

For I love to be her Sunshine,
  Each bright or weary day;
I wonder if it's dark for her
  When I am gone away.

I would not like to live alone
  In the blue sky, like the sun;
Maybe he knows some shining star
  He calls his little one.

I cannot tell just what they mean,
  I'd like to if I could,
When they call me Little Sunshine,
  I guess it's being good.

MAKE OTHERS. HAPPY.

———◆◆———

CHILDREN, do you love each other?
    Are you always kind and true?
Do you always do to others
    As you'd have them do to you?

Are you gentle to each other?
    Are you careful, day by day,
Not to give offense by actions
    Or by anything you say?

Little children, love each other;
    Never give another pain;
If your brother speaks in anger,
    Answer not in wrath again.

Be not selfish to each other;
    Never spoil another's rest;
Strive to make each other happy,
    And you will yourselves be blest.

Bessie's Christmas.

———◆———

LITTLE BESSIE hung her stocking
    Close beside her little bed,
Then, while many funny fancies
    Flitted through her little head
Of the one who was to bring her
    Pretty gifts and pleasant things,
Sleep came gently down, and 'round her
    Closely wrapped his fleecy wings.

In the morning when she wakened,
    Would you really like to know
What so deeply she found hidden
    In the stocking's very toe?
Many things she found before it—
    Many beautiful and bright—
And she said, " I thank you, Santa,
    For remembering me last night."

Folded in a dainty paper,
    All the other things below,
Lay a heart of whitest sugar
    In the stocking's tiny toe.
Folded with it, neatly printed,
    So a little girl might read,
Were the words that every Bessie
    Ought most carefully to heed :

" Strive to keep your heart, my darling,
    Evermore as pure as this,
So your life, when it is finished,
    Will be crowned with perfect bliss.
Far from every evil-doing,
    See that it may always be,
And from evil thought and feeling
    Try to keep it ever free ! "

HAPPY NEW YEAR.

HAPPY New Year, Happy New
Year; oh, send it afar,
To the girls and the boys, wherever they
are.
To the rich and the poor, to the high
and the low;
Oh! scatter its blessings wherever you
go.

Happy New Year, dear children, whose
homes are so bright;
Happy New Year to you whose hearts
are so light;
Happy New Year—oh, say it to all who
can hear,
It will cost you but little—*some* hearts it
may cheer.

Happy New Year to those whose joys
are but few;
Happy New Year, my darlings—God
sends it to you.

(24)

Some days may be dark; but there's
    One ever near
Who bids you rejoice in a happy New
    Year.

Happy New Year, Happy New Year,
    begin it aright;
Ask Jesus to help you—both morning
    and night,
And oft in the day let your little hearts
    pray
To Jesus, the Saviour, who takes sin
    away.

Happy New Year, dear children, oh,
    help make it so;
If you see those in sorrow, go comfort
    them, go;
Sometimes just a word is all their hearts
    crave;
Go tell them of Jesus, and tell them
    he'll save.

THE LOST CHILD.

THE chill November day was done,
    The working world home-faring;
The wind came roaring through the
    streets,
    And set the gas-lights flaring;
And hopelessly and aimlessly
    The seared old leaves were flying,
When mingled with the sighing wind,
    I heard a small voice crying.

And shivering on the corner, stood
    A child of four or over,
No cloak nor hat her small, soft arms,
    And wind-blown curls to cover.
Her dimpled face was stained with tears;
    Her round blue eyes ran over;
She cherished in her wee, cold hand,
    A bunch of faded clover.

(26)

And one hand round her treasure, while
  She slipped in mine the other;
Half-scared, half-confidential, said,
  "Oh! please, I want my mother."
"Tell me your street and number, pet;
  Do n't cry, I'll take you to it."
Sobbing, she answered, "I forget,
  The organ made me do it.

"He came and played at Milly's steps,
  The monkey took the money.
And so I followed down the street,
  The monkey was so funny.
I've walked about a hundred hours,
  From one street to another;
The monkey's gone, I've spoiled my
    flowers,
  Oh! please, I want my mother."

"But what's your mother's name and what
  The street? now think a minute."
"My mother's name is mamma dear—
  The street—I can't begin it."

" But what is strange about the house,
    Or new, not like the others ? "
" I guess you mean my trundle-bed—
    Mine and my little brother's.

" Oh, dear ! I ought to be at home,
    To help him say his prayers ;
He's such a baby he forgets,
    And we are both such players ;
And there's a bar between to keep
    From pitching on each other,
For Harry rolls when he's asleep ;
    Oh, dear ! I want my mother."

The sky grew stormy ; people passed,
    All muffled, homeward faring ;
" You'll have to spend the night with me,"
    I said, at last despairing.
I tied a 'kerchief round her neck—
    " What ribbon's this, my blossom ? "
" Why, don't you know ? " she smiling
        asked,
    And drew it from her bosom.

A card, with number, street, and name,
  My eyes astonished met it;
" For," said the little one, " you see
  I might sometime forget it;
And so I wear the little thing
  That tells you all about it;
For mother says she's very sure
  I would get lost without it."

GOOD-NIGHT, good-night, my little
        one!
All nature sleeps, the day is done!
The lily now has closed its cup,
The violet buds are folded up,
Let not my little one take fright
When mother whispers her good-night;
When mother's arms shall loose their hold,
The Saviour's will more closely fold;
Thy guardian angel he will be,
And never say " good-night " to thee !

Sign The Pledge.

I KNEW a bright and noble youth,
  With fair, unsullied name,
In wandering from the path of truth,
  Go down to death and shame.

When warned by friends of danger near,
  And urged by them to sign,
He turned a cold and listless ear,
  And tarried at the wine.

" He never would a drunkard be,
  He knew just when to stop—
Ne'er sign away his liberty,
  Nor take another drop."

But ah! strong drink made him a slave
  To appetite so base,—
Too late, alas! for him to save—
  A sad and hopeless case.

(30)

A few brief years of want and woe,
   While loved ones o'er him sighed,
He went the way all drunkards go,
   For without hope he died.

Dear youths, from this a warning take,
   Nor sip at wine or beer,
Not even for a lady's sake,
   Though urged by one most dear.

Now come, dear friends, both great and
      small,
   A solemn promise make,
And pledge ye to abstain from all
   That can intoxicate.

A PLEDGE we make, no wine to take;
   Nor brandy red to turn the head.
  To quench our thirst, we'll always bring
  Cold water from the well or spring;
  So here we-pledge perpetual hate
  To all that can intoxicate.

Jesus' Seat.

FAR, far away o'er the deep blue
    sea,
Lived a man who was kind as kind
    could be.
He loved little children, and spread every
    day
A table from which none went hungry
    away.
Poor children came in from the alley
    and street,
With rags on their backs, and no shoes
    on their feet;
Girls and boys, large and small, some
    naughty and rude,
But John Falk loved them all, and did
    them all good.
And while they were eating, he often
    would tell
Of the Lord Jesus Christ, who on earth
    did once dwell;

How he loved little children—each one
    of them there
He was watching from Heaven with
    tenderest care—
And how happy and blessed would be
    the child's part
Who would let that dear Saviour come
    dwell in his heart.
Each day, when the children assembled
    to eat,
He taught them to offer this grace for
    their meat:
" Bless, Jesus, the food thou hast given
    us to-day,
And come and sup with us, dear Jesus,
    we pray."

But once, when the children had finished
    this prayer,
One poor little fellow stood still by his
    chair
For a moment, then ran to the closet
    where stood
The bright cups of tin and the platters
    of wood.

"Now what is the matter?" said Falk
    to the child.
The little one looked in his kind face,
    and smiled:
" We asked the Lord Jesus just now in
    our grace
To sup with us here; but we've left him
    no place.
If he should come in, how sad it would
    be!
But I'll put him a stool close here be-
    side me."

Then the boy, quite contented, sat down
    to his food;
He was hungry and tired, and his supper
    was good!
But a few moments after, he heard at
    the door
A knock low and timid, one knock and
    no more.
He started to open it, hoping to meet
The Lord Jesus Christ come to look for
    his seat;
But when it was open he no one could
    see

But a poor little child, much poorer than
    he,
His face blue with hunger, his garments
    so old,
Were dripping with rain, and he shiv-
    ered with cold.
" Come in ! " cried the boy, in a tone of
    delight,
" I suppose the Lord Christ could not
    come here to-night,
Though we asked him to come and par-
    take of our bread,
So he's just sent you down to us here
    in his stead.
The supper is good, and we'll each give
    you some,
And tell the Lord Christ we are glad
    you have come."

From that time, when the children as-
    sembled to eat,
There was always one place called " the
    Lord Jesus' seat."
And the best that they had was placed
    there each day

For one who was poorer and hungrier
    than they.
And the Lord Jesus Christ, in reply to
    their grace,
Sent always some person to sit in his
    place;
And sweet was the food that the Lord
    did provide
For the stranger he sent them to eat at
    their side.

Dear friends, who have read this short
    story, you know
The words that our Saviour once spake
    when below,
If we wish for his presence to hallow our
    bread,
We must welcome the stranger he sends
    in his stead.
When we set out our feasts, this our
    motto must be—
"As ye do to my poor, ye have done
    unto me."

MARY'S PRAYER.

"WHAT shall I do? what shall I do?"
    the wicked father said,
As in agony of spirit he rose up from
    his bed,
And earnestly entreated his wife to kneel
    and pray;
Alas! dear Mary's mother had ne'er
    been taught the way.

"I cannot pray, dear husband," the
    trembling wife replied;
"Oh, then, what can I do?" in bitter-
    ness he cried.
"Perhaps," she said, "our Mary has
    learned to say her prayers,
She seems so good and holy." They
    hastened up the stairs,

Where slept that young disciple, a child
    of seven years.
Her father gently woke her; then, burst-
    ing into tears,
He said, " Oh ! can you pray, my child ?
    has Jesus taught you how ?
And will you try to pray for your poor
    father now ?"

She knelt, put up her little hands, " Our
    Father up in Heaven,"
She sweetly said, " for Jesus' sake, let
    father be forgiven ;
Have mercy, blessed Saviour ! wash all
    his sins away,
And send the Holy Spirit to teach him
    how to pray."

That father rose in penitence; sweet
    thoughts within him stirred,
A yearning, warm desire to hear from
    God's own word

Those precious truths she thus had lisped
    in accents sweet and mild:
He placed the Bible in her hand—" Take
    this and read me, child!"

She read the holy Book, and at that
    midnight hour
God sent his blessed Spirit to seal it
    home with power.
Those sweet words of the loving John
    that " all who look may live,"
He heard, and said, " Dear Mary, can
    Jesus now forgive?"

" O listen, father. God *so* loved, he
    sent his only Son,
And all who now believe in that dear,
    blessed One—
The Lamb of God—shall not be lost, but
    have their sins forgiven,
And he will take them home, at last, to
    dwell with him in Heaven."

"That is for me!" he cried, "for sin-
    ners just like me;
I will look up to Jesus now—Saviour,
    I come to thee:
I hear those blessed words, Come unto
    me and live;
I can believe—I do believe! Dear Jesus,
    now forgive!"

Yes; look to Christ, believing one, he
    whispers now you may.
He heard, and went from that glad hour,
    rejoicing on his way!

WHO'S the gentle little girl
    Everybody loves to know?
She it is whose heart and thoughts
    Are as pure as whitest snow!
She it is who, meek and good,
Daily grows like Christ the Lord.

THE SUNBEAM.

A DARLING little infant
　　Was playing on the floor,
When suddenly a sunbeam
　　Came through the open door;
And striking on the carpet,
　　It made a little dot;
The darling baby saw it,
　　And crept up to the spot.

His little face was beaming
　　With a smile of perfect joy,
As if an angel's presence
　　Had filled the little boy;
And with his tiny finger,
　　As in a fairy dream,
He touched the dot of sunshine,
　　And followed up the beam.

(41)

He looked up to his mother,
  To share his infant bliss;
Then stooped and gave the sunbeam
  A pure, sweet baby kiss.
O Lord, our Heavenly Father,
  In the fullness of my joy,
I pray that childlike feeling
  May never leave the boy.

But in the days of trial,
  When sin allures the youth,
Send out thy light to guide him,
  The sunbeams of thy truth.
And may his heart be ever
  To thee an open door,
Through which thy truths, as sunbeams,
  Make joy upon life's floor.

WHAT THE ECHO SAID.

ONCE on a time, two little boys,
    And naughty ones you'll say,
Resolved before they'd go to school
    That they would go and play.

The pleasant spot at which they chose
    To seat themselves and chat,
Re-echoed, or sent back the voice,—
    But they did not know that.

Said William to his brother Dick,
    " We shall not be found out."
But Echo mocked the naughty boy,
    And answered, " *Be found out.*"

" I fear," said Dick to little Will,
    " That some one overhears ; "
He looked to see, and Echo then
    Cried, " *Some one overhears.*"

"Oh! never mind," brave Will replied,
  "Come, do not be afraid!"
So when they both began to play,
  Said Echo—"*Be afraid!*"

"What can it be?" said William, then,
  "Oh, let us go to school,"
For he began to be afraid;
  Said Echo—"*Go to school.*"

Then, softly whispering, they said,
  "Oh, if our master knows;"
But Echo, answering every word,
  Said, softly,—"*Master knows.*"

"What shall we do!" then William said,
  "We must not tell a lie."
And then they heard the Echo's voice
  Say—"*Must not tell a lie.*"

So Dick began to cry, and said,
  "William, you brought me here."
Said Echo, in a mournful tone, -
  "*William, you brought me here!*"

"I never will do this again
    If master will forgive,"
Said Will to Dick; and then the voice
    Said—"*Master will forgive!*"

"Then let us go," said little Will;
    "Come, Dicky, do not cry;"
And in the same tone Echo said,
    "*Come, Dicky, do not cry.*"

"We shall not be so very late,
    If we make haste away;"
And Echo, with a warning voice,
    Cried out—"*Make haste away.*"

Then Dicky dried his tears, and said,
    "I will do so no more;"
And Echo, in a cheerful voice,
    Then said—"*Do so no more.*"

"Then we'll be off to school," said they:
    And off they quickly ran,
And, happily, were just in time,
    Before the school began.

Remember, then, my little friends,
   Though Echo nothing knew,
There's One above who always knows,
   Both what you say and do.

JOHNNY'S BOOTS.

A TIMID little shoeless boy
      Plodded along the way
That led through fields and led through
      woods
   To Sabbath-school one day.

There rows of happy children sat,
   And heard the story sweet,
How once in boyhood's simple guise,
   Christ walked with human feet.

And of the little rows of feet
   That hung from benches there,

All were in buttoned boots arrayed,
  But his alone were bare.

He tried to keep them out of sight,
  And blushed with fear and shame
When questioned whence he came and
    why,
  And asked his age and name.

But when the week came round again,
  The shoeless little feet
Brought Johnny with contented face,
  And helped him climb his seat.

Grave, earnest words the teacher spoke,
  On sacred aim intent,
But on the children's faces saw
  Nothing but merriment.

While little hands and smiling eyes
  Said, " Teacher, do look there—
Just look at Johnny's feet, and see
  How soiled and black they are!"

"Dear Johnny," said the teacher, while
   She found it hard to speak
Without a smile, "do wash your feet
   Before you come next week."

Poor Johnny! Disappointed tears
   Came rushing to his eyes;
He looked at his bare feet with shame
   And sorrowful surprise.

"Why, them was clean!" he cried,
    "but as
   I came to school to-day,
I saw a lot of walnut trees
   Growing along the way;

"I climbed up one, and with green nuts,
   And with some juicy roots,
I stained 'em till I thought you'd all
   Think I'd got buttoned boots!"

Now smiles gave way to laughter loud,
   It spread from seat to seat,

Till every child had looked at John—
   Looked at his shoeless feet.

But thoughtless mirth gave way before
   The accents of surprise
With which the teacher bade them look
   At Johnny's weeping eyes;

And drew the grieved and frightened
     child
   Within a kind embrace,
And wiped with tender hands, the tears
   From off his burning face.

Ah, Johnny! you need paint no more,
   Your feet with nuts and roots,
For one who was a boy like you
   Will give you buttoned boots!

WHAT THE MINUTES SAY.

WE are but minutes: little things,
    Each one furnished with sixty
      wings,
With which we fly on our unseen track,
And not a minute ever comes back.

"We are but minutes: each one bears
A little burden of joys and cares;
Take patiently the minutes of pain,
The worst of minutes cannot remain.

"We are but minutes: when we bring
A few of the drops from pleasure's spring,
Taste their sweetness while yet you may,
It takes but a minute to fly away.

"We are but minutes: use us well,
For how we are used we must one day tell.
Who uses minutes has hours to use;
Who loses minutes whole years must lose,"

THE LITTLE SPARROW.

I AM only a little sparrow,
  A bird of low degree;
My life is of little value,
  But the dear Lord cares for me.

He gave me a coat of feathers—
  It is very plain, I know,
With never a speck of crimson,
  For it was not made for show.

But it keeps me warm in winter,
  And it shields me from the rain;
Were it bordered with gold or purple,
  Perhaps it would make me vain.

And now that the spring-time cometh,
  I will build me a little nest,
With many a chirp of pleasure,
  In the spot I like the best.

(53)

I have no barn nor store-house,
   I neither sow nor reap;
God gives me a sparrow's portion,
   But never a seed to keep.

If my meal is sometimes scanty,
   Close picking makes it sweet;
I have always enough to feed me,
   And "life is more than meat."

I know there are many sparrows—
   All over the world we are found;
But our Heavenly Father knoweth
   When one of us falls to the ground.

I fly through the thickest forest,
   I light on many a spray;
I have no chart nor compass,
   But I never lose my way.

And I fold my wings at twilight,
   Wherever I happen to be;
For the Father is always watching,
   And no harm will come to me.

I am only a little sparrow,
　　A bird of low degree;
But I know the Father loves me—
　　Have you less faith than we?

BEARING INJURIES.

WHEN for some little insult given,
　　My angry passions rise,
I'll think how Jesus came from Heaven,
　　And bore his injuries.

He was insulted every day,
　　Though all his words were kind;
But nothing men could do or say
　　Provoked his heavenly mind.

Not all the wicked things he heard
　　Against the truths he taught,
Excited one reviling word,
　　Or one revengeful thought.

And when upon the cross he bled,
  With all his foes in view,
" Father, forgive them," Jesus said,
  " They know not what they do."

Dear Saviour, may I learn of thee
  My temper to amend ;
And, walking in humility,
  May peace my steps attend.

I'M glad my blessed Saviour
    Was once a child like me,
To show how pure and holy
    His little ones might be.
And if I try to follow
    His footsteps here below,
He never will forget me,
    Because he loved me so.

God Sees Me.

I'M not too young for God to see:
　　He knows my name and nature too;
And all day long he looks at me,
　　And sees my actions through and
　　through.

He listens to the words I say,
　　He knows the thoughts I have within:
And whether I'm at work or play,
　　He's sure to know it if I sin.

Oh, how could children tell a lie,
　　Or cheat in play, or steal, or fight,
If they remembered God is nigh,
　　And has them always in his sight?

So when I want to do amiss,
　　However pleasant it may be,
I'll always strive to think of this,—
　　" I'm not too young for God to see."

The White Dove.

SHALL I tell a story, darling?
    I know one, very old;
For when I was a little child
    I used to hear it told.
It is about a little boy,
    And the pigeons which he sold.

His mother she was very poor,
    And kept a rich man's gate;
Until the carriages passed through,
    There Jacob had to wait.

Now Jacob was a patient lad,
    A loving, faithful son;
Of all the things the rich man had
    He wanted only one,—

A pigeon with a crested head,
    And feathers soft as silk,

(58)

With crimson feet and crimson bill,
  The rest as white as milk.

He had some pigeons of his own,
  He loved them very well;
But then his mother was so poor,
  He reared them all to sell.

He kept them in a little shed
  That sloped down from the roof;
Great trouble had he every spring
  To make it water-proof.

He used to count them every day,
  To see he had them all;
They knew his footstep when he came,
  And answered to his call.

And one—a chocolate-colored hen—
  Was prettier than the rest,
Because there was a gloss like gold
  All round its throat and breast.

You know the little birds in spring
  Build houses where they dwell,

And feed and rear their little ones,
　And love each other well.

So the black pigeons Jacob had
　Were mated with the gray;
And crested-crown and ring-neck made
　Their nest the first of May.

The Lord has made each little bird
　To love and need a mate;
And so the little chocolate hen
　Was very desolate.

And Jacob thought if he could get
　The rich man's milk-white dove,
And keep it always for his own—
　Now, listen to me, love;

He wanted that which was not his,
　That which another had;
And so a great temptation grew
　Around the little lad.

The rich man had whole flocks of birds,
　And Jacob reasoned so:

" If I should take this one white dove,
  How could he ever know ?

" Among so many, can he miss
  The one which I shall take ?
Among so many, many birds,
  What difference can it make ? "

But, darling, even while his heart
  Throbbed with these wishes strong,
A something always troubled him—
  He knew that it was wrong.

So time passed on ; he watched the dove—
  How every day it came
Nearer and nearer to the shed,
  More gentle and more tame.

He watched it with a longing eye ;
  At last one summer day,
He saw it settle on the roof,
  As if it meant to stay.

Now Jacob seemed a happy boy ;
  Said he, " It has a right

To choose a dwelling anywhere
   Most pleasant in its sight."

And so he scattered grains of corn
   And crumbs of wheaten bread,
Because he thought the dove would stay
   Where it was kindly fed.

As time passed on, the milk-white dove,
   Well pleased with Jacob's care,
Soon learned to know him like the rest,
   And seemed right happy there.

One morning he had called them all
   Around him to be fed,
And on the ground he scattered corn,
   And peas, and crumbs of bread.

When, all at once, he heard a man
   Outside the road-gate call,
" Boy, if these pigeons are for sale,
   I think I'll take them all."

Ah! how it smote on Jacob's ear!
   " I see there are but eight;

If you will take eight shillings down,
    I'll pay you at that rate."

Now, at that moment, all the birds
    Were feeding in the sun,
But Jacob, in his startled heart,
    Could think of only one.

And never since the milk-white dove
    Had joined the chocolate hen,
Had he felt in his inmost heart
    As he was feeling then.

" Come—hurry, hurry," said the man ;
    " I have no time to lose ;
Between the shillings and the birds
    It can't be hard to choose."

Poor Jacob, having once begun
    To do what was not right,
Forgetting he was standing in
    His Heavenly Father's sight,

And knowing how his mother had
    A quarter's rent to pay,

Felt in his heart the sense of right
  Was fading fast away;

When from the open cottage door
  There came a murmuring low:
It was his mother's morning hymn,
  Solemn, and sweet, and slow.

He listened, and a holy fear
  Was wakened in his heart,
And strength was given him that hour
  To choose the better part.

Then, turning to the stranger man
  A frank, untroubled eye,
He said, " But seven birds are mine;
  But seven you can buy."

" Oh ! " said the man, " they go in pairs,
  And will not suit me then ; "
So Jacob sold him only six,
  And kept the chocolate hen.

And when the evening shadows came,
  And dew was on the grass,

He watched outside the garden-gate,
    To see the rich man pass;

Close to his breast the milk-white dove
    He held with gentle care,
While many a soft caress he laid
    Upon its feathers fair.

And when at last the rich man came,
    Poor Jacob, rendered bold
By feeling he was in the right,
    His artless story told.

Then, after he had owned to all
    The wrong which he had done,
And the worst wrong he wished to do,
    He lifted to the sun

A happy, open, fearless face,
    Which won the rich man's love,
Who kindly bade him always keep
    For his, the milk-white dove.

Soon Jacob, once more good and true,
    Stood in his mother's sight,

The struggle of temptation past,
  The wrong all turned to right,

And with his troubled heart at rest
  Lay down upon his bed;
And whiter wings than his white dove's
  Were round his pillow spread.

LITTLE THINGS.

A GRAIN of corn an infant's hand
   May plant upon an inch of land,
Whence twenty stalks might spring, and
    yield
Enough to stock a little field.

The harvest of that field might then
Be multiplied to ten times ten,
Which, sown twice more, could furnish
    bread
Wherewith an army might be fed.

A penny is a little thing,
Which e'en a poor man's child may bring
Into the treasury of Heaven,
And make it worth as much as seven.

As seven! yea, worth its weight in gold
And that increased a hundred-fold;
For lo! a penny tract, if well
Applied, may save a soul from hell.

That soul can scarce be saved alone—
It must, it will its bliss make known;
" Come," it will cry, " and you shall see
What great things God hath done for me."

Hundreds that joyful sound shall hear—
Hear with the heart as well as ear,
And those to thousands more proclaim
Salvation in the only name.

TELLING FORTUNES.

"Be not among wine-bibbers; among riotous eaters of flesh; for the drunkard and the glutton shall come to poverty, and drowsiness shall clothe a man with rags."—Prov. 23: 20, 21.

I'LL tell you two fortunes, my fine
    little lad,
  For you to accept or refuse;
The one of them good, and the other one
    bad—
  Now hear them, and say which you
    choose.

I see by my gifts, within reach of your
    hand,
  A fortune right fair to behold,—
A house and a hundred good acres of land,
  With harvest-fields yellow as gold.

I see a great orchard, the boughs hanging
    down
  With apples of russet and red;

(68)

I see droves of cattle, some white and
    some brown,
  But all of them sleek and well fed.

I see doves and swallows about the barn
    doors,
  See the fanning-mill whirling so fast ;
See men that are threshing the wheat on
    the floors ;—
  And now the bright picture is past !

And I see, rising dismally up in the place
  Of the beautiful house and the land,
A man with a fire-red nose on his face,
  And a little brown jug in his hand !

Oh, if you beheld him, my lad, you would
    wish
  That he were less wretched to see ;
For his boot toes they gape like the mouth
    of a fish,
  And his trousers are out at the knee !

In walking he staggers now this way, now
    that,
  And his eyes they stand out like a
    bug's ;

And he wears an old coat and a battered-
     in hat,
     And I think that the fault is the jug's.

For the text says the drunkard shall come
     to be poor,
     And that drowsiness clothes men with
       rags ;
And he does n't look much like a man, I
     am sure,
     Who has honest hard cash in his bags.

Now which will you choose ? to be thrifty
     and snug,
     And be right side up with your dish ;
Or to go with your eyes like the eyes of
     a bug,
And your shoes like the mouth of a fish ?

LOVE ONE ANOTHER.

 A LITTLE girl, with a happy look,
  Sat slowly reading a ponderous
   book,
All bound with velvet and edged with
  gold,
And its weight was more than the child
  could hold ;
Yet dearly she loved to ponder it o'er,
And every day she prized it more,
For it said—(and she looked at her smil-
  ing mother)—
It said, "Little children, love one an-
  other."

She thought it was beautiful in the book,
And the lesson home to her heart she
  took ;
She walked on her way with a trusting
  grace,
And a dove-like look on her meek young
  face,

Which said, just as plain as words can
    say,
"The Holy Bible I must obey;
So, mamma, I'll be kind to my darling
    brother,
For little children must love each other.

"I'm sorry he's naughty, and will not
    play,
But I'll love him still, for I think the way
To make him gentle and kind to me,
Will be better shown, if I let him see
I strive to do what I think is right.
And thus, when I kneel in prayer to-night,
I will clasp my arms around my brother,
And say, 'Little children, love one an-
    other.'"

The little girl did as her Bible taught,
And pleasant indeed was the change it
    wrought;
For the boy looked up in glad surprise
To meet the light of her loving eyes;
His heart was full, he could not speak,
But he pressed a kiss on his sister's cheek,
And then looked up to the happy mother,
Whose little children loved one another.

HARRY'S ADVICE.

SAID Jennie, "Tell me, mamma, please,
   When I'll be old enough
To wear my hair in puffs and curls,
   And frizzles out so rough?

"I'd like to use the crimping-pins,
   Wear pearls and jewels fine;
How soon shall I be old enough?
   Oh, dear! I'm only nine.

"And, mother dear, why may I not
   Wear corsets, like Aunt Jane?
And great, long, dangling earrings, too,
   And dresses with a train?

"And pretty little flattering vails,
   That make one look so fair?
And feathers in my bonnet, too,
   All fluttering in the air?"

"Why need I always be a child,
    And go to bed at eight?
Aunt Jennie sits up every night,
    So very, very late.

"What's well for her, I am quite sure,
    Would be as well for me;
Now try it, mother, just this once,
    And see how good I'll be."

Then Harry, three years older, spoke;
    He felt so wondrous wise,
He thought to make the matter plain,
    And watch her quick surprise:

"Why, sis, you're foolish; don't you
        know
How terrible it is
When little girls to women grow,
    And wear their hair afriz?

"How all your flossy curls must change,
    So harsh and straight to grow?

They'll burn your hair and sear your head,
　With irons hot, you know.

" They'll prick your little shell-like ears
　With a needle's biting sting;
And squeeze your plumpness all away
　With an awful corset string.

" And should you sit up late, you'd have
　Such dreadful dreams at night,
You'd cry to be a child again,
　Or for morning's golden light.

" And then, you know, you could n't run,
　Nor slide with me down hill;
Now think it over, and decide
　To be my playmate still."

" O Harry, Harry, is it true?
　Must ladies suffer so?
Oh, dear! what can a poor child do?
　I hope I'll *never* grow."

BEWARE OF THAT TRAP.

LET me tell you a tale of a little gray
mouse,
That had left his snug nest at the top of
the house
To cut capers and play on the old kitchen-
floor,
Where he danced with delight for ten
minutes or more.

But at last little mousey, while rolling a
ball,
Caught sight of a box standing close to
the wall—
Such a snug little box, with its half-open
door,
And its windows of wire behind and be-
fore.

So he looked and he longed for that mor-
sel of cheese
Which he saw on the floor; he could get
it with ease;
(76)

And then he'd go home to his nest (so
    he thought,
Silly mouse!). He went in; the door
    shut—he was caught.

You are in, little mousey; but how to
    get out
Is a question you never need trouble
    about;
You may peep through the bars, and
    tremble, and wait,
Till the trap is unsprung and you meet
    with your fate.

O my boy! you may laugh at the poor
    little mouse;
But my tale has a moral—keep far from
    the house
Where temptation assails you, and riot-
    ous brawl;
*The public-house bar is the trap by the
    wall.*

A Sign-Board.

I WILL paint you a sign, rum-seller,
   And hang it over your door;
A truer and better sign-board
   Than ever you had before.
I will paint with the skill of a master,
   And many shall pause to see
This wonderful piece of painting,
   So like the reality.

I will paint yourself, rum-seller,
   As you wait for that fair young boy,
Just in the morning of manhood,
   A mother's pride and joy.
He has no thought of stopping,
   But you greet him with a smile,
And you seem so blithe and friendly,
   That he stays to chat awhile.

I will paint you again, rum-seller,
   I will paint you as you stand,
(78)

With a foaming glass of liquor
  Extended in your hand;
He wavers, but you urge him,
  Drink, pledge me just this one,
And he takes the glass and drains it,
  And the hellish work is done.

And I next will paint a drunkard;
  Only a year has flown,
But into this loathsome creature
  The fair young boy has grown.
The work was sure and rapid,
  I will paint him as he lies
In a torpid, drunken slumber,
  Under the wintry skies.

I will paint the form of the mother,
  As she kneels at her darling's side,
Her beautiful boy that was dearer
  Than all the world beside.
I will paint the shape of a coffin,
  Labeled with one word—"lost."
I will paint all this, rum-seller,
  And will paint it free of cost.

The sin and the shame and the sorrow,
　　The crime and the want and the woe,
That is born there in your workshop,
　　No hand can paint, you know.
But I'll paint you a sign, rum-seller,
　　And many shall pause to view
This wonderful swinging sign-board,
　　So terribly, fearfully true.

LEARN TO SAY NO.

YOU'RE starting, my boy, on your
　　　　journey
　　Along the highway of life;
You'll meet with a thousand temptations,
　　Each city with evil is rife;
This world is a stage of excitement,
　　There's danger wherever you go;
But if you are tempted in weakness,
　　Have courage, my boy, to say no!

The bright ruby wine may be offered:
  No matter how tempting it be,
From poison that stings like an adder,
  My boy, have courage to flee.
The billiard saloons are inviting,
  Decked out with their tinsel and show;
If you should be tempted to enter,
  Think twice—then stoutly say no!

In courage alone lies your safety;
  When you the long journey begin,
Your trust in a Heavenly Father
  Will keep you unspotted from sin.
Temptations will go on increasing,
  As streams from a rivulet flow;
But if you'd be true to your manhood,
  Have courage, my boy, to say no!

Poems. 6

DISOBEDIENCE.

BY the gate of the garden near the
    wood,
A brother and sister together stood.
"Beyond the gate you are not to roam,"
Their mother had said, as she quitted
    home;
But, tired of playing within the bound,
Frank opened the gate, and they looked
    around;
"O Jessie," he cried, "how I long to go
To play for awhile in the wood below!"

"But, Frankie, what did our mother
    say?"
Said the little one, tempted to go astray.
"She thought in the wood we might be
    harmed,"
Said Frank, "but we need not be alarmed;
There is nothing to hurt us; and oh!
    just see
That beautiful squirrel on yonder tree!"

And away ran Frank to the green retreat,
While Jessie followed with flying feet.
They chased the squirrel with laugh and
    shout,
They gathered the flowers and played
    about,
And then, as they feared it was getting
    late,
Returned unhurt to the garden gate.
No questions were asked, and nobody
    knew
What Frank and Jessie had dared to do,
Till Saturday night, as they sat alone,
Frank to his mother the truth made
    known.

" But, mother," he said, " though we went
    in the wood,
We got no harm, as you thought we
    should;
Into the water we did not fall,
Nor did we injure our clothes at all."
" My son," was the answer, " it may be so,
Yet something you lost in the wood, I
    know;

Think well, and then tell me," the mother
    said,
As she laid her hand on Frankie's head.

" My knife, my ball, and my pence,"
    thought he,
" I have them all safe—and what could
    it be ?
I know," at length he said with a start,
" I have lost the happy out of my heart !
I have not felt easy since then," he sighed,
" And I could not be merry, although I
    tried.
Mother, I'm certain not all my play
Made up for the loss that I had that day."

Frank's tears fell fast as the summer rain,
But the happy came back to his heart
    again,
As he to his mother his fault confessed,
And her pardoning kiss on his lips was
    pressed.
Dear children, remember this simple lay,
For if in forbidden paths you stray,
Though you seem unhurt, and your fault
    be hid,
You will lose a treasure, as Frankie did.

LITTLE KNUD.

"NOW go, little Knud," said his
    mother,
  "Ere yet the sun is low;
For the road is long to the pasture,
  And you must drive home the cow."
"I'm going, good-by, dear mother,"
  The willing child replied;
"On the road I will not linger,
  Nor play by the river-side."

With his heart aglow with the sunshine
  Of his mother's parting smile,
His face serene as a summer's sky,
  His conscience free from guile,
He went forth; and the loving Saviour
  Who watched him along his way,
Only knew it was a martyr child
  Going forth to die that day.

He watched the glistening wheatfields
    Swaying before the breeze,
His heart in tune with the merry birds
    Singing among the trees;
" God has made all things in beauty,"
    He thought, with a swelling heart,
" I will be thy child, my Saviour,
    And never from thee depart."

He came, at length, to the river-side;
    " Those are wicked boys, I know;
I'll pass them without a word," thought
        Knud,
    But they would not let him go.
" Stay," they said, " the apples are ripe!
    We'll have some, and you shall go, too."
" Oh, no! 't would be stealing," the boy
        replied,
    " And that I cannot do."

" Stay," cried the rough, bad boys again,
    " Nay, but you must and shall;
You'll pick the fruit for us to eat,
    So climb over the garden wall."

In fearless tone, Knud made reply,
    And his words were right and pure,
" I cannot steal, I would rather die,
    I never will steal, I'm sure."

" We'll see now whether he speaks the
       truth,"
    And their faces were dark with wrath,
As they seized the frightened, struggling
       boy,
    And bore him down the path.
They bore him to the water-side,
    " We'll plunge you into the flood,
If you do not our bidding now."
    " I cannot steal," said Knud.

They plunged him down, they held him
       there ;
    " You shall die," they said, " or yield ; "
And evil angels, crowding near,
    Their hearts to pity steeled.
They drew him up and asked again,
    " Are you ready *now* to go ? "

The little hero gasped for breath,
   And bravely answered, " No."

They threw him from them into the flood,
   And he sank in the watery bed ;
That frightened, throbbing heart was still,
   For the martyr child was dead.
All night the stricken parents sought
   For the precious, lifeless clay ;
All night they toiled, but found it not
   Until the break of day.

Then over the land the story flew,
   And many a cheek turned pale,
And filled with wonder many a heart
   To hear the sorrowful tale.
And many a Christian mother prayed,
   With a chastened, trembling joy,
" May the spirit rest on our children dear,
   Of the brave Norwegian boy."

[The incident related above occurred in the
vicinity of Chicago some twenty-three years ago.
The lad was only ten years old, and his name
was Knud Iverson.]

"I Can't" and "I'll Try."

THERE were two little sisters, Luella
    and Bell,
  In their persons no difference you'd spy,
But Luella endeavored to do all things
    well,
  While Bell would not even try.

If a difficult task were proposed by their
    aunt,
  One might always foretell the reply;
Bell would always drawl out a languid,
    "I can't,"
  While Luella would answer, "I'll try."

If a new piece of music to either were
    sent,
  Why, Bell would at once lay it by,
Say, "I'm sure I can't learn it," and rest
    quite content
  That Luella should take it and try.

A church they both sketched from a copy
 well drawn,
  And each made the tower awry;
" I can't do it straight," Bell exclaimed,
 with a yawn;
  But Luella still said, " I will try."

Now, which of these girls do you think
 would excel?
  I am sure you will instantly cry,
" Not the languid, inactive, and indolent
 Bell,
  But Luella, who always would try."

Let all, then, who wish to be happy and
 wise,
  With zeal to their duties apply;
If the sad words, " I can't," to their lips
 should arise,
  Let them change them at once for " I'll
 try."

Industry and Idleness.

A WASP met a Bee on his travels
  one day,
And he paused for a moment, good morn-
  ing to say;
Then added, "I wish you would tell me,
  my dear,
Why people regard me with horror and
  fear!

"Ah! you need not look sorry, and shake
  your wise head,
You know that my presence is greeted
  with dread.
If I buzz round the windows, the ladies
  will cry,
And the children all shout, 'O that *wasp!*
  it must die!'

"Deliberate murder is stamped on each
  face,
And really for *me* there is no resting-place;

(91)

'Tis surely no wonder your family thrive,
When men all stand ready to build you
    a hive.

" I do not make honey for others to sell,
But I eat and I like it, you know very
    well.
We resemble each other—although it is
    true
That I have more gold round my person
    than you.

" We speak the same language, we sing
    the same song,
Though your body is stout while mine is
    quite long;
And my waist is more taper, my clothes
    such a fit,
While my sting is much stronger, as you
    will admit ! "

" Oh ! that is the trouble," then answered
    the Bee,
" And makes a vast difference between
    you and me.
I'm busy all day, and so keep on the wing,
That, laying up sweets, I forget I can sting.

" For clothes that are fine and for jewelry
    rare,
I have not the time to arrange, I declare.
And I frankly confess I am in such haste,
I never once thought of the size of my
    waist.

" I like to be useful, for I've understood
That even an insect is here for some good.
You'll own, my dear friend, there is great
    satisfaction
In leading a life of industrious action."

" Good-by," said the Wasp, as he turned
    up his nose,
And buried himself in the heart of a rose;
" I'd take your advice, I am sure, if I could,
But it's late in the day for a *Wasp* to be
    good ! "

The moral, I think, little children, is clear:
If you wish to be happy, be useful while
    here.
Take care of the moments, for swiftly
    they go,
And you must be storing up honey, you
    know.

Giving Thanks.

A LITTLE boy had sought the pump
   From whence the sparkling water
      burst,
And drank with eager joy the draught
   That kindly quenched his raging thirst;
Then gracefully he touched his cap—
   "I thank you, Mr. Pump," he said,
"For this nice drink you've given me!"
   (This little boy had been well bred.)

Then said the Pump, "My little man,
   You're welcome to what I have done;
But I am not the one to thank—
   I only help the water run."
"Oh, then," the little fellow said
   (Polite he always meant to be),
"Cold Water, please accept my thanks,
   You have been very kind to me."

" Ah ! " said Cold Water, " do n't thank
    me ;
Far up the hillside lives the spring
That sends me forth, with generous hand,
    To gladden every living thing."
" I'll thank the Spring, then," said the boy,
    And gracefully he bowed his head.
" Oh, do n't thank me, my little man,"
    The Spring in silvery accents said.

" Oh, do n't thank me—for what am I
    Without the dew and summer rain ?
Without their aid I ne'er could quench
    Your thirst, my little boy, again."
" Oh, well, then," said the little boy,
    " I'll gladly thank the Rain and Dew."
" Pray do n't thank us—without the sun
    We could not fill one cup for you."

" Then, Mr. Sun, ten thousand thanks
    For all that you have done for me."
" Stop ! " said the Sun, with blushing face,
    " My little fellow, do n't thank me ;

'T was from the ocean's mighty stores
 I drew the draught I gàve to thee."
" O Ocean, thanks!" then said the boy—
 It echoed back, " Not unto me—

" Not unto me, but unto Him
 Who formed the depths in which I lie,
Go, give thy thanks, my little boy,
 To Him who will thy wants supply."
The boy took off his cap, and said,
 In tones so gentle and subdued,
" O God, I thank thee for this gift;
 Thou art the Giver of all good."

PEEPING over yonder mountain,
 See the brilliant orb arise;
Dazzling suns in every fountain
 Meet our beauty-loving eyes.
Fragrant odors rise to meet us—
 Nature's incense to her King—
Cheerful insects fly to greet us,
 While the praise of God they sing.

THE NEW BONNET.

A FOOLISH little maiden bought a
    foolish little bonnet,
With a ribbon and a feather, and a bit
    of lace upon it;
And that the other maidens of the little
    town might know it,
She thought she'd go to meeting the next
    Sabbath just to show it.

But though the little bonnet was scarce
    larger than a dime,
The getting of it settled proved to be a
    work of time;
So when 't was fairly tied, all the bells had
    stopped their ringing,
And when she came to meeting, sure
    enough, the folks were singing.

So this little foolish maiden stood and
    waited at the door;
And she shook her ruffles out behind, and
    smoothed them down before.

"Hallelujah! hallelujah!" sang the choir
    above her head,—
"Hardly knew you! hardly knew you!"
    were the words she thought they said.

This made the little maiden feel so very,
    very cross
That she gave her mouth a twist, her
    little head a toss;
For she thought the very hymn they
    sang was all about her bonnet,
With the ribbon, and the feather, and
    the bit of lace upon it.

And she would not wait to listen to the
    sermon or the prayer,
But pattered down the silent street and
    hurried up the stair,
Till she reached her little bureau, and in
    a bandbox on it
Had hidden safe from critic's eye her
    foolish little bonnet.

Which proves, my little maidens, that
    each of you will find
In every Sabbath service but an echo of
    your mind;

And that the little head that's filled with
    silly airs,
Will never get a blessing from sermons
    or from prayers.

THE ROBIN'S LECTURE.

I HEARD a bird lecture one morning,
    this spring,
And 't was this that he said almost the
    first thing:
"I've been off for awhile where the win-
    ters are warm,
But now have come back, and am preach-
    ing Reform.

"I have heard other lecturers say I would
    find
It a very hard thing to enlighten the
    mind;
But, nevertheless, my success I shall try,
All over the country, wherever I fly."

And his musical voice through the old
    orchard rang,
For the lecture I speak of a sweet robin
    sang;
"Oh! do not feel hurt," this he said in
    his song,
"But I very much fear you have been
    brought up wrong.

"Do open your windows and let in the
    air,
I know you'll feel better and look far
    more fair—
Now, just look at me, why, I never take
    cold;
And in excellent health I expect to grow
    old."

Then he stepped back and forth on the
    limb of the tree,
But I knew all the while he was looking
    to see
If what he had said my attention had
    caught,
And made the impression upon me it
    ought.

And then he went on, " I have known in
    my day
A great many birds all reared the same
    way ;
Their cradles were rocked to and fro by
    the breeze,
And the roofs of their houses were leaves
    of the trees.

" But I never have known a birdling to
    droop,
Nor, old as I am, seen a case of the
    croup—
Nor heard a bird say that so sore was his
    throat
That he, for his life, could not raise the
    eighth note.

" And one with dyspepsia, too gloomy
    to sing,
That we should consider a terrible thing ;
Consumption has never unmated a
    pair "—
Here the bird commenced warbling an
    ode to fresh air.

"Our habits are good, and our natures
  are quiet,
We hold but one error, and that's in our
  diet;
We love grain and fruit, but now and
  then eat
(I might as well own it) a tidbit of meat.

"We lave in the brook, and we drink
  nothing strong
(If I'd time I would sing you a 'cold
  water song'),
And when earth's great lamp has gone
  out in the west,
You'll find our lays hushed, and our bod-
  ies at rest.

"We birds are so happy, but I must not
  stay,
For sev'ral appointments await me to-
  day."
Then he stepped back and forth on the
  limb of a tree,
And flew out of sight wishing long life to
  me.

Discontent.

DOWN in a field, one day in June,
    The flowers all bloomed together,
Save one, who tried to hide herself,
    And drooped, that pleasant weather.

A robin, who had soared too high,
    And felt a little lazy,
Was resting near a buttercup,
    Who wished she was a daisy.

For daisies grow so trig and tall;
    She always had a passion
For wearing frills about her neck
    In just the daisies' fashion.

And buttercups must always be
    The same old tiresome color,
While daisies dress in gold and white,
    Although their gold is duller.

"Dear robin," said this sad young flower,
　"Perhaps you'd not mind trying
To find a nice white frill for me,
　Some day when you are flying?"

"You silly thing!" the robin said;
　"I think you must be crazy!
I'd rather be my honest self
　Than any made-up daisy.

"You're nicer in your own bright gown;
　The little children love you;
Be the best buttercup you can,
　And think no flower above you.

"Though swallows leave me out of sight,
　We'd better keep our places;
Perhaps the world would all go wrong
　With one too many daisies.

"Look bravely up into the sky,
　And be content with knowing
That God wished for a buttercup
　Just here where you are growing."

Only a Spark.

A LITTLE spark on the hearth-stone
    lay,
  Glowing and ruddy and bright;
The ashes around were cold and gray,
  And nobody thought that night,
That the spark would cause such sorrow
    and loss,
And burn from the church to the market
    cross.

But Lady Wind, who was out for fun,
  Peeped in through the window pane;
"There's a spark," she said, "and only
    one,
  I'll blow it into a flame.
There'll nobody burn, for they've firemen
    now,
And I feel like doing it anyhow."

But every door and lattice was tight,
  Not a chink the wind could find.

"Oh! very well," said the mischievous
  wight,
  "Chimneys are quite to my mind.
Though dirty and dark the way I must
  go,
There'll be light enough when I get be-
  low."

Then down she went, and the spark she
  blew,
  She blew it into a blaze;
The house was burnt, and the fire still
  grew,
  The city was in a craze.
And many a home still carries the mark
Of sorrow and loss from that little spark.

There are little sins, my children dear,
  Like little sparks they lie;—
Oh! do not think "there is nothing to
  fear"—
  You must crush them till they die,
Or else they will grow and grow like flame,
And make of your life a ruin and shame.

BEAUTY.

BEAUTIFUL faces, they that wear
 The light of a pleasant spirit there,
It matters not if dark or fair.

Beautiful hands are they that do
The work of the noble, good, and true,
Busy for them the long day through.

Beautiful feet are they that go
Swiftly, to lighten another's woe,
Through summer's heat or winter's snow.

Beautiful children, if rich or poor,
Who walk the pathways sweet and pure,
That lead to the mansions strong and sure.

THE BEST THAT I CAN.

———◆———

"I CANNOT do much," said a little
   star,
  "To make the dark world bright!
My silvery beams cannot struggle far
   Through the folding gloom of night.
But I'm a part of God's great plan,
And I'll cheerfully do the best I can."

"What's the use," said a fleecy cloud,
   "Of these few drops that I hold?
They will hardly bend the lily proud,
   Though caught in her cup of gold.
But I'm a part of God's great plan,
So my treasure I'll give as well as I can."

A child went merrily forth to play;
   But a thought, like a silver thread,
Kept winding in and out all day
   Through the happy, golden head:
   (110)

" Mother said, darling, do all you can,
For you are a part of God's great plan."

She knew no more than the glancing star,
    Or the cloud with its chalice full,
How, why, and for what all strange things
      are,
    She was only a child at school;
But she thought, " It is part of God's
      great plan
That even I should do all I can."

She helped a younger child along
    When the road was rough to the feet,
And she sang from her heart a little song
    That we all thought passing sweet;
And her father, a weary, toil-worn man,
Said, " I will do likewise the best that I
      can."

DISTRUST.

I TRIED to cheer the little girl,
　　And told her "not to mind,"
But still she sobbed, while her bright eyes
　　With gushing tears were blind.

The playmate she had loved the best,
　　And lovingly believed,
Had broken her fond trust, and so
　　The little girl was grieved.

Some secret Mary Lisle had learned
　　From little Isabel,
And, hearing it, she gave her word
　　That she would never tell;

But ere the errant breath of eve
　　To sighs the leaves had stirred,
She, deeming promises light things,
　　Repeated every word.

(112)

'T would truly be a trivial thing
 That little ones should weep
O'er broken faith, did not their hearts
 Such recollections keep.

When cold and wintry are the days,
 The gayest birds take wings;
Time takes a pleasant memory,
 And leaves a thought that stings.

So, little girl, if you have wronged
 Another by your deeds,
Remember that some little heart
 In silent anguish bleeds.

And Mary Lisle's accustomed smile
 No more to Isabel
Was beautiful, " for she had told,"
 Yet promised " not to tell."

And little Isabel went forth
 More cautious on her way;
Afraid to trust her little friends
 Lest some one might betray.

God loves the true and faithful heart,
    And notes the truth above;
And God is grieved whenever here
    Distrust outcasteth love.

MAY'S NEW YEAR'S WISH.

ERE the tripping feet of dawn
      Chased the light and led the
        morn,
Little May, in haste to rise,
Opened wide her laughing eyes.
Brushing, with a gentle grace,
Tangled curls from off her face,
Noiselessly she found her way
Where her mother sleeping lay.
"Happy New Year, mother dear!"
    Breathed she in the loved one's ear;

" Happy New Year, pa, for you !
　Little baby brother, too ! "
　Quickly then her eyes of blue
　Very, very thoughtful grew ;
　Then she drew close to the bed,
　And in softest accents said,
" Mother, will not Jesus listen
　If I send one up to Heaven ? "
　When the mother gave assent,
　On the carpet low she bent,
　And exclaimed, with joy absorbed—
" Wish you Happy New Year, Lord ! "
　Then she said, with beaming brow,—
" I'll be good the whole year now ;
　That I know's the only way
　To make Him happy every day."

　Little children, would n't you
　Like to make Him happy too ?
　Then you must, like little May,
　Be good children *every day*.

CHRISTMAS EVE.

— ♦ —

'TWAS the eve before Christmas:
   "Good-night" had been said,
And Annie and Willie had crept into
   bed;
There were tears on their pillow, and
   tears in their eyes,
And each little bosom was heaving with
   sighs,
For to-night their stern father's com-
   mand had been given,
That they should retire precisely at
   seven,
Instead of at eight; for they troubled
   him more
With questions unheard of than ever be-
   fore;
He had told them he thought this delu-
   sion a sin,
No such being as "Santa Claus" ever
   had been,

And he hoped, after this, he should
nevermore hear
How he scrambled down chimneys with
presents each year.
And this was the reason why each little
head
So restlessly tossed on the soft, downy
bed.

Eight, nine, and the clock on the steeple
tolled ten ;
Not a word had been spoken by either
till then,
When Willie's sad face from the blanket
did peep,
And he whispered, " Dear Annie, is you
fast asleep ? "
" Why no, brother Willie," a sweet voice
replies,
" I've tried all in vain, but I can't shut
my eyes,
For somehow it makes me so sorry be-
cause
Dear papa has said there is no 'Santa
Claus.'

Now we know there is, and it can't be
    denied,
For he came every year before mamma
    died;
But then I've been thinking that she
    used to pray,
And God would hear everything mamma
    would say,
And perhaps she asked him to send
    Santa Claus here
With the sack full of presents he brought
    every year."
" Well, why tan't we p'ay dest as mamma
    did then,
And ask God to send him with presents
    aden ? "
" I've been thinking so, too."   And
    without a word more,
Four little bare feet bounded out on the
    floor,
And four little knees the soft carpet
    pressed,
And two tiny hands clasped close to each
    breast.

" Now, Willie, you know we must firmly
    believe
That the presents we ask for we're sure
    to receive.
You must wait just as still, till I say the
    ' Amen,'
And by this you will know that your turn
    has come then.
Dear Jesus, look down on my brother
    and me,
And grant us the favors we're asking of
    thee.
I want a wax dolly, a tea-set, and ring,
And an ebony work-box that shuts with
    a spring;
Bless papa, dear Jesus, and cause him to
    see
That Santa Claus loves us far better
    than he;
Do n't let him get fretful and angry again
At dear brother Willie and Annie.
    Amen."
" Please, Desus, 'et Santa Taus tum
    down to night,
And b'ing us some p'esents before it is
    light.

I want he sood dive me a nice 'ittle s'ed
With b'ight shinin' 'unners, and all
    painted 'ed;
A box full of tandy, a book and a toy,
Amen, and den Desus, I'll be a dood boy."
Their prayers being ended, they raised
    up their heads,
And with hearts light and cheerful, again
    sought their beds.
They were soon lost in slumber both
    peaceful and deep,
And with fairies in dreamland were roam-
    ing in sleep.

Eight, nine, and the little French clock
    had struck ten,
Ere the father had thought of his chil-
    dren again;
He seems now to hear Annie's half-
    suppressed sighs,
And to see the big tears stand in Willie's
    blue eyes;
"I was harsh with my darlings," he
    mentally said,
"And should not have sent them so early
    to bed.

But then I was troubled; my feelings
found vent,
For bank-stock to-day has gone down ten
per cent.
But of course they've forgotten their
troubles ere this,
And that I denied them the thrice-
asked-for kiss;
But just to make sure, I'll steal up to
the door,
For I never spoke harsh to my darlings
before."
So saying, he softly ascended the stairs,
And arrived at the door to hear both of
their prayers.
His Annie's "bless papa" draws forth
the big tears,
And Willie's grave promise falls sweet
on his ears.
"Strange, strange I'd forgotten," said he,
with a sigh,
"How I longed, when a child, to have
Christmas draw nigh.
I'll atone for my harshness," he inwardly
said,   [in my bed."
"By answering their prayers ere I sleep

Then he turned to the stairs, and softly
    went down,
Threw off velvet slippers and silk dress-
    ing gown,
Donned hat, coat, and boots, and was out
    in the street,
A millionaire facing the cold, driving
    sleet.
Nor stopped he until he had bought
    everything,
From a box full of candy to a tiny gold
    ring.
Indeed, he kept adding so much to his
    store,
That the various presents outnumbered
    a score.
Then homeward he turned with his holi-
    day load,
And with Aunt Mary's help in the nurs-
    ery 't was stowed.
Miss Dolly was seated beneath a pine
    tree,
By the side of a table, spread out for
    her tea.

A work-box well filled, in the center
    was laid,
And on it the ring for which Annie had
    prayed.
A soldier in uniform stood by a sled,
"With bright shining runners, and all
    painted red."
There were balls, dogs, and horses, books
    pleasing to see,
And birds of all colors were perched in
    the tree,
While Santa Claus, laughing, stood up
    in the top,
As if getting ready more presents to drop.
And as the fond father the picture sur-
    veyed,
He thought, for his trouble, he'd amply
    been paid;
And he said to himself, as he brushed
    off a tear,
"I'm happier to-night than I've been
    for a year;
I've enjoyed more true pleasure than
    ever before;
What care I if bank-stock fall ten per
    cent more?

Hereafter I'll make it a rule, I be-
    lieve,
To have Santa Claus visit us each Christ-
    mas Eve."
So thinking, he gently extinguished the
    light,
And tripped down the stairs to retire
    for the night.
As soon as the beams of the bright morn-
    ing sun
Put the darkness to flight, and the stars
    one by one,
Four little blue eyes out of sleep opened
    wide,
And at the same moment the presents
    espied.
Then out of their beds they sprang with
    a bound,
And the very gifts prayed for were all of
    them found.
They laughed and they cried in their in-
    nocent glee,
And shouted for "papa" to come quick
    and see

What presents old Santa Claus brought
    in the night,
("Just the things that we wanted") and
    left before light.
"And now," added Annie, in a voice soft
    and low,
"You'll believe there's a Santa Claus,
    papa, I know."
While dear little Willie climbed up on
    his knee,
Determined no secret between them
    should be,
And told in soft whispers, how Annie
    had said,
That their blessed mamma, so long ago
    dead,
Used to kneel down and pray by the side
    of her chair,
And that God, up in Heaven, had an-
    swered her prayer.
"Then we dot up and prayed dest as
    well as we tould,
And Dod answered our prayers. Now
    was n't he dood?"

"I should think that he was, if he sent
　　you all these,
And knew just what presents my chil-
　　dren would please.
Well, well, let him think so, the dear
　　little elf,
'T would be cruel to tell him I did it
　　myself."
Blind father! Who caused your stern
　　heart to relent,
And the hasty words spoken so soon to
　　repent?
'T was the Being who bade you steal
　　softly up stairs,
And made you his agent to answer their
　　prayers.

Sabbath Readings,

FOR THE HOME CIRCLE.

——:o:——

Volumes 1 and 2 each contain 400 pages of

Moral & Religious Reading

For the household; carefully compiled for the use of
Sabbath-School and Family Libraries.

——:o:——

Price of each Volume, 60 Cents.

Golden Grain Series,

A CHOICE COLLECTION OF

INSTRUCTIVE STORIES,

ILLUSTRATED AND

☞ Beautifully Bound in Two Volumes. ☜
PRICE, $1.00.

Vol. 1, THE HARD WAY, 160 pp.,   -   50 cts.
Vol. 2, THE SCHOOL-BOY'S DINNER, 160 pp.,   50 cts.
Other Volumes in preparation.

The same reading in Ten Pamphlets of 32 pages each,
without pictures.

Price, 50 Cents.

Address,   **REVIEW & HERALD,**
Battle Creek, Mich.